Quartzsite Arizona

No Ordinary Place

A Mini-History
by
LELAND FEITZ

With Photographs by
Billie Casey

LITTLE LONDON PRESS
716 E. Washington
Colorado Springs, Colorado 80907

ISBN 0-936564-01-6

*Dedicated to my sister
Maxine Adams
who first introduced me
to Quartzsite*

INTRODUCTION

During the winter of 1978, I visited Quartzsite for the first time. I was back again in 1979 and again in 1980. I liked the place! I had never seen anything quite like it with this mass of people drifting in for the winter only to drift on again in the spring. I began to wonder about the Quartzsite that was there before the "snowbirds" found it.

This lead to my reading everything I could find about the place and conversations with Quartzsite people. Then, I found in Billie Casey someone who could help me with my facts and photos about the place. Here then, is our combined effort.

This is not intended to be a complete history of this remarkable little Arizona town. Instead, it is in the form of a salute to a place Billie and I both have a deep feeling for — she as one who lives there permanently, and I as one who visits it occasionally.

Leland Feitz
October, 1980

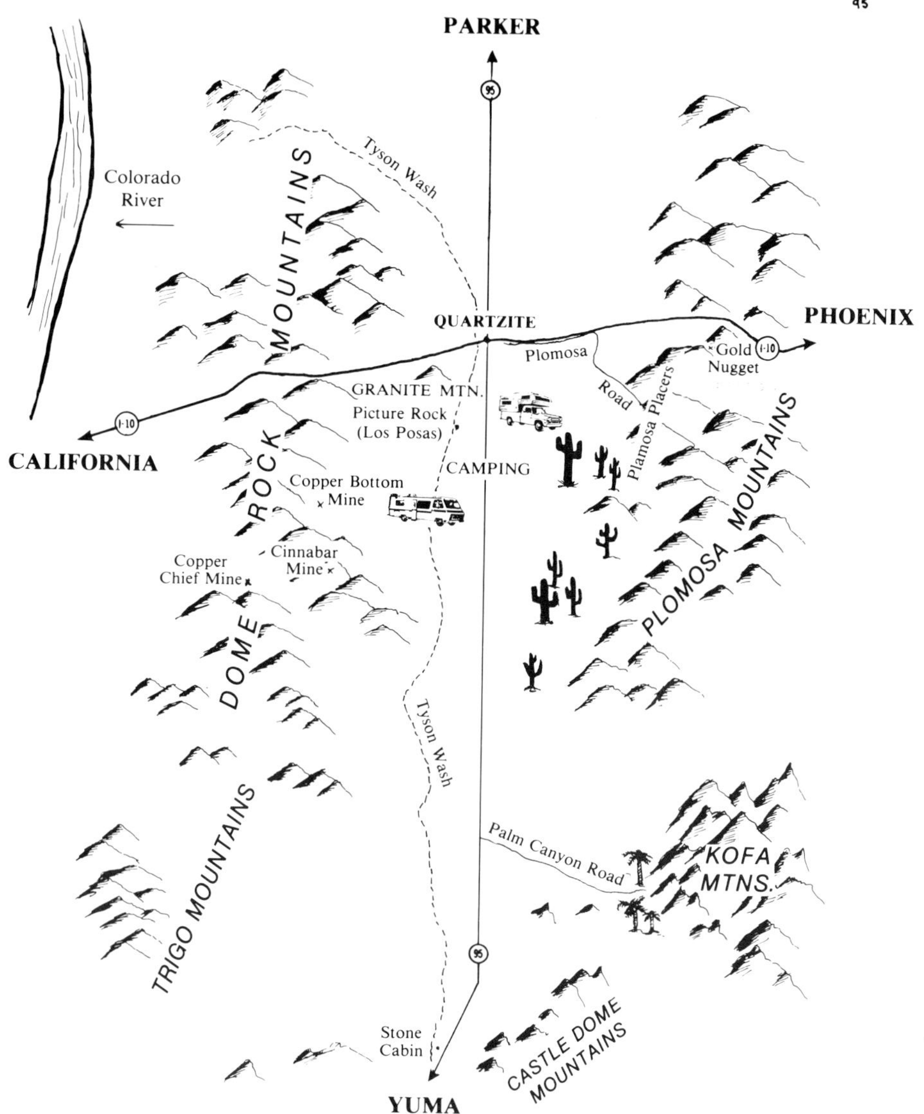

PARKER
95
Colorado River
Tyson Wash
MOUNTAINS
QUARTZITE
Plomosa
PHOENIX
Gold Nugget
I-10
GRANITE MTN.
Picture Rock
(Los Posas)
Plomosa Placers
Road
CAMPING
I-10
CALIFORNIA
Copper Bottom
Mine
ROCK
PLOMOSA MOUNTAINS
Copper
Chief Mine
Cinnabar
Mine
DOME
TRIGO MOUNTAINS
Tyson Wash
Palm Canyon Road
KOFA MTNS.
95
Stone Cabin
CASTLE DOME MOUNTAINS
YUMA

Quartzsite, Arizona, No Ordinary Place

When the "snowbirds" return to their northern homes each spring, little Quartzsite once again becomes the sleepy Arizona desert town it has really always been. Then, some 600 full time residents relax from the busy winter season and ready themselves for the blazing hot summer, the season many of them like best.

"Sure it gets hot here," said one native," but after the winter rush and after that mass of people who come here for the Pow Wow, it's kind of nice to enjoy the quiet of the place. A Quartzsite grocer added, "The winter people make it possible for us to live here all year, and that is exactly what we want to do. Stopped here on our way to California 18 years ago. We liked the place and never went on."

An Oklahoma woman, who moved to Quartzsite with her husband about 20 years ago, had this to say: "Once in awhile a bunch of us who have moved here over the years get together, and we usually ask each other this question. 'What was it that made us fight so like hell to get to this damn place?' "

One does wonder. For, on a first visit there, Quartzsite does not look as if it would be a very livable place. It sits in the middle of a desert, sort of in the middle of nowhere. Being an unincorporated town without much in the way of zoning controls, it has grown in a haphazard sort of way. As with most small towns, there are little groups who fuss with other little groups and not much goes on but what everybody in the whole place knows about it. While it is growing, it still isn't big enough to have many of the advantages that come with town living. And it sure gets hot!

But let's scratch a little deeper. There is a lot more to be said *for* Quartzsite than can be said against it.

While it does get hot there during the summer months, Quartzsite's climate during the other seasons is just about perfect. The air is crystal clear and totally unpolluted. And, while Quartzsite may sit in the middle of nowhere, that is part of its charm. The open desert and the mountains which surround the place are absolutely magnificent, especially in the spring when they are blanketed with a myriad of lovely wild flowers. The Quartzsite country is littered with a variety of semi-precious rocks and minerals to delight the collector. Back roads lead to fascinating old ghost towns and mining camps. Hiking trails probe into the vast land even more deeply. There are interesting desert creatures to observe and to hunt.

The Colorado River some 20 miles away, offers fine fishing and boating. The river scenery to the north, between Parker and Lake Havasu City, becomes spectacular, and the recreational opportunities are almost unlimited. It's not terribly far from there on to Las Vegas. Los Angeles and San Diego are both about a half a day's drive from Quartzsite. Palm Springs and California's desert playgrounds are much closer. Phoenix can be reached by car in a little more than two hours. Yuma, Quartzsite's county seat, is 80 miles to the south, and it offers most of the advantages of city life. San Luis, Sonora, a major gateway to Mexico, is just another 23 miles away.

The location for exploring the southwest is perfect. This adds much to the pleasure of wintering and living in Quartzsite.

There is still much more to be said for this town. Being unincorporated and not having too many rules, there is a freedom unknown by most city people. Here, the people do their own thing without much interference from a system or from neighbors. Quartzsite is a community of free spirits!

"There are a few sons-a-bitches here," one oldtimer explained, "but for the most part we are mighty fine people." Even during a casual visit one does get the feeling that Quartzsite's permanent residents are among the friendliest people to be found just about anywhere. Most of them have considerable pride in this wide spot by the side of Interstate 10. But, there are some who don't. A woman transferred there by her employer several years ago said, "You don't live in this damn town. You just exist."

Quartzsite's economy depends almost totally on tourism. Each winter, this "poor man's Palm Springs" as Yuma writer Frank Love calls it, swells to a community of some 12,000. Free parking for recreational vehicles in mammoth desert campgrounds just south of town is one of the big attractions, especially for retired persons who are living on limited incomes.

The winter weather there is almost perfect, and most people who drift into the desert country from harsh climates in the north feel better under Arizona's warm sun. Quartzsite's low elevation (879 feet) and its clean, dry air help to make others more comfortable.

A local man who has profited from the winter boom said, "There's no doubt about it. This town has been helped by arthritis and inflation." Now, don't think for one minute that Quartzsite is just a community of older people who are there for health and budget reasons. Indeed not! While those are valid reasons for spending a winter in Quartzsite, most people go there because they have a very good time.

"I've been coming down here by myself every winter for the last five or six years," said an older woman from Colorado, "and, I don't know of any place I'd rather be. I live in my little camper out on the desert but I'm in town dancing two or three times a week. We have such good times here. . . . Have you seen our wonderful Civic Center?"

The building she spoke of, with a value of well over $200,000 was constructed mostly by winter people who simply gave of their time and talent. Developed and directed by the amazing Quartzsite Improvement Association, the building houses a winter recreational program which offers something for everyone, seven days a week.

Up to 600 persons turn out for the Saturday night dances. There is no admission, but a "kitty" is on the stage with the 17-piece Hi Jolly Music Makers. On Sunday people gather in the same place for a worship service. On Sunday night, the hall fills up again. This time it's for square dancing!

During the week, the Civic Center's craft rooms fill with happy people pursuing their interests and hobbies. Others are in Spanish classes or learning about the desert or Arizona history.

There are bingo nights, imported entertainments and more dancing. On Wednesday evenings, the big, modern dining hall fills up for the weekly pancake supper. As many as 440 show up for that. Over 1500 attend the lively holiday dinners. "Potluck affairs", the turkey and ham is supplied by the Quartzsite Improvement Association. Volunteers decorate the huge hall and scores of tables and plan appropriate programs.

It's not all play. Many of the winter people busy themselves with profitable hobbies. An amazing mix of people, they are a creative bunch who manage to stay busy even in retirement away from their regular homes. Many have their lapidary equipment set up alongside their mobile homes and spend their days making lovely jewelry items from rocks picked up on desert outings. Ironwood, picked up from the same place, is turned into beautiful carvings by talented hands. Painters work on pretty desert scenes. Many of the things created there ultimately find their way into regional arts and crafts shows, including Quartzsite's own Pow Wow.

It is the Pow Wow, of course, for which little Quartzsite is best known. A gem and mineral show of immense proportions, it is an annual February event. Rockhounds gather there from all over the world. Some 30,000 campers and trailers park in the desert around town and for a few days, Quartzsite becomes one of the biggest cities in Arizona.

Sponsored by the Quartzsite Improvement Association, income from the Pow Wow has been used to improve the quality of life in the city hosting it. The Civic Center, focal point of the now international show, has been improved. There is a fine, new clinic. QIA funds have also been used to update the Fire Department and the library.

While Quartzsite has great appeal to the snowbirds and rockhounds, it has other fans too. During weekends, when the weather is mild, Quartzsite and the open land surrounding it serves as a haven for adventurous families from the big cities of California. An increasing number of young people, especially geology students, zip into town in vans loaded with sleeping bags and camping equipment to pick up supplies for desert and mountain explorations.

Being at the point where Interstate 10 crosses US 95, Quartzsite serves a trickle of travelers all year long. Except for the winter, however, it is a pretty quiet place.

As early as 1856, this spot was something of a watering hole for cross country travelers. A few wells there provided water for a stage stop between the Colorado River port city of LaPaz and, later Ehrenberg and Prescott. Called Tyson Wells Stage Station, it was named for Charles Tyson. A simple adobe building, it served those who traveled this desert route as late as into the 1880's.

A compound of several buildings and commonly called "Ft. Tyson," the place resembled a fort though it really never was one. Even so, the place did serve as a regular stop for US Army troops traveling between Ehrenberg and Prescott. It may also have provided some protection to both travelers and settlers from the threat of Indian conflicts.

Martha Summerhayes, a military wife who traveled extensively in Arizona during the mid-1870's, wrote about Tyson Wells Stage Station in her delightful book, *Vanished Arizona*. In part, she said, ". . . it reeks of everything unclean, morally and physically. . . ."

A post office was established there in 1893 with Michael Welz as postmaster. In only two years, it was deserted. It was simply called Tyson's.

The "fort" ultimately became the Oasis Hotel. While not exactly posh it nevertheless offered shelter from the weather and food and drink for those passing through.

A settlement, located some two miles south of the present town of Quartzsite, at a place called Picture Rock had water which supplied a handful of settlers and the few prospectors who passed that way. The area was probably settled permanently as early as 1860, though petroglyfs on nearby rocks indicate the place was used by a much earlier people.

Picture Rock was washed away in 1870 when a cloudburst simply swept the little settlement off the face of the earth, and burying forever, it is claimed, one Mexican merchant's safe containing some $50,000 and a good bit of expensive jewelry. Leaving that place, the people set up their new community near Tyson Wells.

It wasn't until 1896, however, that a second post office was established there. The name Quartzite had been suggested owing to the abundance of that rock found in the immediate area. According to one report, however, the Post Office Department made a mistake, added an "s" making the official name Quartzsite. The postmaster was George Ingersoll, and the post office was located on Moon Mountain Road.

Between the time the people moved in from Picture Rock until shortly after the post office was established, miners from LaPaz, Ehrenberg and other desert outposts converged on the spot which was to grow into Quartzsite. Something of a supply center, there was a hotel, butcher shop, general store and quite a few saloons.

While there was gold, silver, copper and other ore bodies in the mountains surrounding Quartzsite, and while they were probed thoroughly by early prospectors, few real bonanzas were struck close by.

Only the Cinnabar, Copper Bottom and Mariquita, Moon Mountain, Gold Nugget Mines get much mention by the more serious regional historians. Of them, the Mariquita has the most interesting past.

The Mariquita was discovered in the late 1880's by a French mining man, Jacque Travis. For some time he worked in the Dome Rock Mountains with a dry washer carried on his back, hardly making a living. One day, by chance, he came upon the lode from which his tiny bits of placer gold had come. Working the claim by himself, he hauled the first load of ore to the Colorado River mill where it brought some $4000. Using part of that money, he went to San Francisco and found himself a wife.

Returning to Arizona, the newlyweds planned on working the mine only until they had accumulated enough money to return to France to live the good life. But only a few days after Travis returned to his Mariquita, he was bitten by a rattlesnake and died. The wife left Quartzsite not to return, though she did realize some wealth from the mine many years later after long court battles.

The Plomosa Placers in the Plomosa Mountains just east of Quartzsite have been the scene of frenzied mining activity off and on since 1872. However, it wasn't until 1880 that the area was worked extensively. At that time a large mining company leased some 3000 acres and put 70 men to work with dry concentraters, which sifted the gravel through screens of varying sizes. Something like one dollar's worth of marketable ore was found in each ton of rock worked through the hand-driven machines. Not much when water was selling for $1.25 a keg!

Dozens of other one and two man operations using dry washers were also to be found in the Plomosas. They, too, stirred up a lot of dust, but not much gold.

Quartzsite enjoyed something of a mild "boom" during the early part of the new century when all Western states were caught up in a wave of mining excitement. At that time Quartzsite boasted of having 10 saloons, one Chinese restaurant, "Greek George's" Barber Shop and a cluster of other little businesses including Sam Wilson's general store. Grand plans were developed for the building of the Congress Mill. But most of them were abandoned and a rather modest stamp mill was built instead.

During the first few years of the 1900's, miners scratched about the hills east and west of town barely making a living. Only about $45,000 worth of ore was reported to have been taken from the Plomosa District during the first 30 years of the new century. Promoters who were selling stock in ''successful Quartzsite mining operations'' in San Francisco were doing a lot better than the miners!

While Quartzsite never became a ghost town, its population was probably well under 100 right after the 1900 ''boom''. Census figures are not available, but only 16 people voted in the 1900 election in Quartzsite. Four years later, 57 people voted. One Wyatt Earp was a candidate for constable. Only 14 voters turned out for the 1908 elections. By 1910, population was up to 339.

In 1930, 112 people lived there. Until the great depression of the 1930's there was not much activity in Quartzsite. But then, hard times brought many desperate men back to the desert with their picks, shovels and dry washers. Working under a scorching hot sun was rough work, but the men were able to pick up a few dollars, and for the proud individual, that beat the big city breadline. One who lived in Quartzsite during the depression remembers, ''You could see little clouds of dust all over the hillsides around here. Quartzsite was really pretty busy at that time. Men drifted in with their bed rolls and a little bit of equipment.''

Over 100 men attempted to make their livings by mining in the Quartzsite hills during 1932 and 1933. The area is believed to have produced ores worth over $176,000 between the early 1930's and 1949.

Mining men are a pretty decent bunch and those who floated in and out of Quartzsite were no exception. They set up what Jack Delaney, a Desert Magazine writer, called a ''pre-social-security-system.'' Actually, it was just an understanding between men. Nothing was promised and nothing was expected. But when a man had a bit of luck and had enough gold to go to town for supplies, it was understood he would share those supplies with his less fortunate neighbor. And he generally did.

For the next few years, ''Sleepy Quartzsite'' slipped into a period of hibernation. By the early 1960's the town's summer population had shrunk to 50, according to Paul Feldman who operated a little lapidary shop there. But, by the first day of January each year, the area's population shot up to about 1500. A trickle of winter people, which was to become a flood, had begun. Quartzsite was about to see its first *real* boom!

Knowing the place was bound to grow as a winter colony, some 44 forward thinking people, mostly new property owners, set out to organize for the future. Their very first meeting was held on the night of March 23, 1965. Then one month later, they met again and the Quartzsite Improvement Association was officially incorporated. Glen Fulton was elected president.

That year and the next, meetings were held in the Sigurd B. Sigrudson home, with members hauling in folding tables and chairs. The meetings were pot-luck affairs followed by card games, slide shows and lively discussions about community concerns. There was always talk about holding some sort of rock and gem show which seemed to be a logical thing for the Association to sponsor. Many of its members were rockhounds, and already little chance meetings of collectors swaping rocks and rock yarns were taking place around town.

After considerable planning, the first official rock and gem show was held in February of 1967. It was staged at the old school house on Moon Mountain Road. There were eight exhibitors in the building and some 20 "tailgaters" in the parking lot. The ladies of the association served coffee and sandwiches. An estimated 1000 people showed up for the three day affair. Quartzsite's first Pow Wow was a success!

By then the Association's membership was up to about 100, mostly winter people. An enthusiastic group, they began talking about building a hall. Sig Sigurdson gave the association four acres of land and helped to finance the construction of the new building. Then a flurry of events ranging from rummage and food sales to card parties took place with the money going for the hall. Mary Allen, QIA historian, recalls the "Halves for the Hall" parties. These were card games with 50 cent admissions.

A shell of a building was completed late in 1967 largely through the generosity of the association's "angel," Sig Sigurdson. President Fulton advanced the association money for materials to complete the necessary interior work. The work itself was all done by volunteers!

On January 11, 1968, the hall, now called the Civic Center, was completed. The members of the association were proud, and they had every right to be. Good people working together had produced something of a desert miracle. That year, of course, the Pow Wow had a new home. Some 100 exhibitors, mostly locals, set up displays in the hall. The four-acre lot surrounding the Civic Center building was parked full of rockhounds swapping rocks with other rockhounds.

During the next year, with money made from the 1968 show and the help of the faithful volunteer organization, the dining room was added to the east side of the main building. In 1969 meals were served there to Pow Wow visitors. That year, some 12,000 people came. There were over 300 exhibitors.

Then tragedy struck. The building burned to the ground. The date was October 8, 1969. The 1970 Pow Wow, with bigger crowds than ever, was held in a makeshift sort of place. By year's end, the entire complex was rebuilt.

By 1973 the association's membership numbered over 500. The money this hard working group of part-time residents generated with the Pow Wow made possible many improvements to the building. The money came from renting display spaces, food service and special projects such as commemorative coins. By this time the show was getting considerable national and even international attention.

Far more than just a rock show, the big hall by now was housing displays of all sorts of lapidary equipment and handcrafted jewelry. There were demonstrations of silversmithing and other related crafts. Publishers were there with their latest books about collecting minerals.

Pow Wow's eighth year, 1974, was the first *really big show.* Parking lot spaces were leased out to some 450 exhibitors 60 days before the show even opened. Million dollar gem displays were set up in the main hall. And some 200,000 people came to Quartzsite! On one day alone, an estimated 90,000 people toured the acres of displays.

As the 1974 show closed, most of the 600 "tailgate" display spaces for the 1975 Pow Wow sold out. They were paid for a full year in advance!

Had any little community with only a part-time population of workers ever pulled off anything quite like this? Probably not. But, hold on. Over 500,000 people came to the Pow Wow in 1975. Then, an estimated 700,000 came in 1976. *Arizona Highways* estimated the 1978 attendance at 750,000. The Yuma County Sheriff's Department suggested as many as 1,000,000 may have passed through Quartzsite during that year's event. Again in 1980, an estimated 750,000 people came to Quartzsite during Pow Wow Week.

Considering its immense size and the tiny size of the host city, it is remarkable that such a massive event runs so smoothly. There have been few incidents to mar the joy of the gathering over its years of existence. There seems to be a comradery among the people that is unique in a gathering of this scope and size.

It is an event which puts many dollars into the economy of the town. Local businesses, busy all winter anyway, are absolutely swamped during the Pow Wow. One to profit most is, of course, the founding Quartzsite Improvement Association. The money it receives is plowed back into its projects.

QIA money built the transmitter which brings television into the area. The Volunteer Fire Department has been equipped with funds from the Association. The Medical Center, too, is the result of the planning and work of the QIA. It sits on land donated by the community spirited group.

From the start, the association was blessed with hard working men and women who gave freely of their time and talents and knew how to get things done. This group and the people who live in Quartzsite full time do not always see eye-to-eye, but the fact remains the association has improved the quality of life in this desert outpost especially for the winter people.

There are those who have not been totally pleased with the success of the annual Pow Wow and they do, indeed, have an understandable view. For the most part, they are old-timers or people who moved to Quartzsite many years ago to escape the problems that accompany growth and population. An editorial in the *Arizona Sunset,* a little paper published in Quartzsite during 1976 put it well:

> "Estimates of the Pow Wow crowd vary from 100,000 to over 1,000,000. Inaccurate to say the least, but there were more people this year than last for sure. Our Quartzsite is a community of about 400 year round residents and a few thousand winter residents, all who like the area and its beauty and climate and its easy going way of life. The explosion each February at the present rate will destroy the beauty, change the climate to a smog-filled terror and turn people away from what was an easy going community."

A valid view. No one would argue that.

Most of the people who come to Quartzsite for the winter live in their own travel homes in one of the free campgrounds or at one of the town's

25 trailer parks. No city, nevertheless, Quartzsite does provide most of the services required by the big influx of winter people.

The town sprawls over quite a large area on both sides of Tyson's Wash. Just as there is an interesting mix of people, so is there an interesting mix of housing. Lovely ranch style homes in well landscaped grounds sit by old and new mobile homes and aged adobes from the last century. Quartzsite's people live on graveled streets with interesting regional names such as Ocotillo, Quail, Ironwood, Camel Mesquite, Roadrunner and one honoring the winter visitor called Snowbird.

There is a nine hole golf course right in the center of town and a fine, small library. Tyson Wells' old stage station is now being restored by the Central Yuma County Preservation Society, Inc. and is well on its way to becoming a museum. There is a scattering of old landmarks, but the big attraction is the grave of Hadji Ali (Hi Jolly) the Arab camel driver. Since the pyramid marking his grave was dedicated by the Governor of Arizona in 1935, this has been one of the most visited spots in the southwest.

Hi Jolly (that is how the foreign name sounded to the desert people) came to the Arizona country from his native Syria during the mid 1850's with a score or more of North African camels. They had been ordered by the United States Army for a desert experiment, and Hi Jolly was hired as chief camel driver.

It was felt the camels would make excellent beasts of burden in this desert country. But, the camels were not compatible with the Army's mules and the whole plan was junked in 1864. On February 26, 1864, 34 camels were auctioned off at Benecia, California and the remaining 66 auctioned off at Camp Verde on March 18, 1866. A few found homes in California Zoos while many were bought by circus' and side shows and eventually turned loose on the desert. Hi Jolly kept a few for himself and attempted to operate a freighting business between Colorado River port cities and the mining camps to the east. Even though the animals could carry up to 600 pounds of goods and travel more than 60 miles a day without water, his plan, like the Army's, did not work out. In 1868, he turned his last camel loose near Gila Bend, Arizona. Hi Jolly then went to work prospecting and doing a little scouting on the side for the government. He died in 1902. His grave, now marked by what has been called the ''centerpiece of the cemetery'', is a large pyramid made of the stones of the Quartzsite country and topped by a little copper camel.

A few steps from Hi Jolly's pyramid is the grave of Judge George Hagley, certainly Quartzsite's best known and most loved pioneer. Born there in the stage station in 1894, he spent his whole useful life in Quartzsite. In 1947, he became the Justice of the Peace, an office he was continuously elected to for eight terms. For most of those years, his office was in his home facing the highway which passed through town. (People drifted in and out of his home at will for a third of the century, making it something of a community gathering place.) Hagely claimed he married over 37,000 couples during his long career including Al Jolson and a number of other celebrities.

Not long before Judge Hagley died in 1977, he spoke about Quartzsite. He said, "We have so many new people up here now. These snowbirds come in from Oregon and up north. They come and they go. I'm practically a stranger here now."

Bill Keiser is buried there, too. This man came to Quartzsite in 1904 and lived there until he died in 1963. Having worked in most of the mines of the region, probably no one knew the Quartzsite country better than Keiser. But, what's important, he wrote it down! Hundreds of pages of his reminiscences concerning his life there fell into the hands of the Yuma County Historical Society. In 1978 many of his very personal stories were published in a booklet called *Bill Keiser's Lost Mines and Prospector's Lore* by the Yuma County Historical Society and the Central Yuma County Preservation Society.

Another monument of interest is that of George Fremont Coné. A dignified memorial there reads: "Dedicated to a kindly desert man, philosopher, woodworker, wise and loyal friend." Coné's ashes were scattered on his beloved desert after a long solitary life there. Something of a "Dr. Doolittle of the Desert", Coné communicated with its creatures as few have been able to do. Not only did this little man survive there, he was totally tuned into it. A thinker and artist, he created lovely carvings from ironwood he picked up on his desert wanderings. His close-up photographs of desert wildflowers were exceptional.

There are graves marked only by slabs which are slowly rotting away. A cluster of little markers stand by a scrubby cactus. One reads: "Martinez Infant 1903-1903. Martinez Twins, 1904-1904. Martinez Infant 1906-1906." Other infants are resting in Quartzsite's cemetery, too. Survival for the very young in an outpost such as this was difficult.

A strange group, it seems, to be sharing a final resting place in the center of a desert. But this mix of people with their greatly differing backgrounds is somewhat symbolic of Quartzsite. No ordinary town, it has always been made up of an extraordinary mix of people who drifted there from the four corners of the world for one reason or another. This is what made Quartzsite unique during its early years and it's what makes the place unique today.

QUARTZSITE, as it was . . .

The miners came
And the miners went
This was the place
Their gold was spent.

"The Quartzsite Symphony" in front of C.B. Genungs Red Front Saloon, 1889. (From the collection of Billie Casey)

A bunch of the boys. Quartzsite business and social leaders, 1907.

Downtown Quartzsite in 1908. The view is east toward the Plomosa Mountains. (1. Hagley Hotel, 2. Sam Wilson's Store, 3. Scott's Store.)

Today one has to watch out for "snowbirds" on Quartzsite's busy Main Street. In earlier times, birds of another kind had to be dealt with.

School days. The little people of little Quartzsite in 1908. Now, Quartzsite's children are bused to Parker, Salome and Eherenburg for their educations.

The Quartzsite Post Office and Sam Wilson's Store in 1915 was the "hub" of the community.

By 1916, Tyson's Wells Stage Station had been rebuilt and was in business as the Oasis Hotel. While not exactly "The Ritz", its thick adobe walls, nevertheless, offered the traveler protection against the desert's heat and cold.

1920 Quartzsite. The view is toward the west and the Dome Rock Mountains.

"Ft. Tyson," later the Oasis Hotel, weathered away to almost nothing before an effort was made to preserve it.

Quartzsite's first post office was at the Ingersoll Mill site on Moon Mountain Road. It was also home of Postmaster George Ingersoll.

Pioneer Quartzsite family, Angela and William Scott owners of Scott's Bar & Grocery with their children, William, Joseph and Phillip.

One of many placer camps outside Quartzsite during the early part of the century. This one belonged to Bill Keiser. Water delivered to such operations, where temperatures reached 127 degrees, was $1.25 a keg.

A dry washer in operation in the Plomosa area east of Quartzsite. Through a dusty process, gravel was sifted until only sand with the promise of gold was left.

QUARTZSITE, as it is . . .

The winter people come
And the winter people go
They sit in the sunshine
And they talk about snow.

Halsey Williams' Mill with Q Mountain in the background. The mill operated between 1940 and 1950.

The remains of the Stetler Stamp Mill at the foot of Q Mountain overlooking Quartzsite.

The home and workshop of Joseph Cone', desert artist, craftsman in ironwood, philospher and friend of many.

The last camp of "Hi Jolly" attracts many visitors each season. Hadji Ali was a camel driver with the famed U. S. Camel Corps created in 1857 by Jefferson Davis, then Secretary of War and later President of the Confederacy.

The Quartzsite jail. A desert hellhole, prisoners were held here until they could be taken to Yuma.

The home of the Hagley family. Their son, George, grew up to become a respected judge and beloved Quartzsite citizen.

Scott's Store and Bar. Built by Quartzsite pioneers W.E. and Angella Scott, the business is now operated by their son, Ben.

Tyson Wells Stage Station is well on its way to becoming a museum. It has been re-built through the efforts of dedicated Quartzsite historians.

The Quartzsite Medical Center opened in 1975 and provides medical service for the people of Quartzsite and the many winter visitors.

Quartzsite Civic Center, a haven for winter visitors was completely rebuilt after fire destroyed the original building on October 8, 1969.

A view of the First Baptist Church new sanctuary, a 50′ × 100″ addition to the church with a seating capacity of 350. Dedication services were held on Feb. 10, 1980.

The 14th Annual Pow Wow sponsored by the Quartzsite Improvement Association drew buyers and sellers from all parts of the USA and several foreign countries.

A sea of sellers on the desert sands, during the annual rock show.   At the Sell-O-Rama.

Young and old find treasures for sale at the annual Gem, Mineral and Hobby Show.

Something for everyone.

*All contemporary photos
by Billie Casey.*

IN APPRECIATION

Without the help of several old and new friends, this little effort could not have been accomplished. I am especially grateful to Mary Allen, Billie Casey, Evelyn Huff, Rose Weber, Norma Kovacik, Steve Mayer and the helpful staffs of the Yuma County Historical Society and the Yuma Public Library.

Leland Feitz